BYGONE IPSTONES

Lindsey Porter

A chunk of bygone Ipstones was uncovered with the refurbishment of the lower canal basin at Froghall in Spring 2004.

BYGONE IPSTONES

Lindsey Porter

CONTENTS

1. VILLAGE AND OTHER SCENES ... 6

2. SOCIAL EVENTS ... 19

3. ALL IN A DAY'S WORK ... 29

4. VANISHED BUILDINGS AND WORKS ... 45

5. THE CANAL ... 55

6. THE RAILWAY ... 64

7. WINTERY REMINDERS ... 71

8. WHEN WE WERE YOUNG ... 74

INTRODUCTION

The idea for this book came from Jodi Peck of Belmont Grange. I had quite a few old photographs of the area, but insufficient for a publication. I was lucky to obtain the majority of the rest from Malcolm and Pauline James together with Roger and Christine Wood. Without their support this book would not have been possible.

The photographs are mainly from the twentieth century, showing fascinating scenes of the village together with others in the neighbourhood. More unusually, several old invoices from various shop keepers etc have been included. They were for purchases by Mr Berisford of White Chimneys Farm, on Ipstones Edge.

There is a good selection of photographs of social events in the village plus a variety of images of school children. I suspect that many readers will recognise family and friends and I hope that these photographs bring back happy memories rather than any sad ones. Although they cover many village activities and events, there are few scenes of the Agricultural Show and the former carnival. Although it would have given a better balance, it would have been at the expense of other views of village social life and I hope my selection is considered in a good light.

I have strayed out of the village in certain chapters, adding details I thought would be of interest. I have also deliberatel avoided naming many people portrayed; the bulk of the photographs in Chapter 2 include too many people.

I have tried to avoid using images which are likely to be covered by copyright, unless I have permission. However, some images do not record the name of the photographer and if I have infringed copyright, I offer my apologies.

I wish to acknowledge the help I have received from various people in compiling this book, especially Margaret Burnett; Emma Hewson; Malcolm & Pauline James; William Podmore and Roger & Christine Wood. If I have forgotten anyone else, please accept my apologies.

Ipstones

June 2009

1. VILLAGE AND OTHER SCENES

Heading for home. The building on the left was the butchers at one time. On the right is Beard's grocers shop and is now a dwelling.

Village and other scenes

The Golden Lion Inn in Froghall Road, later called The Linden Tree. It remained a popular inn and restaurant until Graham and Val Roberts left in April 2007. It has had three different licensees since then and is currently for sale and closed.

Mr Hartley's petrol station and garage (now the Country Store) taken in 1965.

Bygone Ipstones

The Post Office in Edwardian times at the top end of Brookfield Road.

The view of the old school from Brookfield Road.

Village and other scenes

The Marquis of Granby c. 1962-3 which was then a Joules' Brewery (of Stone) inn and the Trading Post was Alexander's shop.

The nearest cottage in Church Lane has had a floor removed and there are now two floors instead of three. Note the milk churns awaiting collection. The church is just visible on the left. Photograph taken 1962–3.

Cottages in Church Lane. The upper photograph is probably Edwardian, with a comparison with 1962–3 (below).

Village and other scenes

The former toll house in the High Street, on the corner of the road to Foxt. The toll house was on the Cheadle – Butterton Moor End turnpike, authorised in 1770. It would appear to be the only one to have survived from this road and has now been extended. Beyond is Mrs Wright's shop.

Another view of the same building, c. 1962-3.

Bygone Ipstones

Sharpcliffe Hall showing three gardeners. This old image is undated.

The Hall's drawing room in 1927, when the house was put up for sale.

Village and other scenes

Above: Between 1946 and 1954 the Hall was a Youth Hostel. Here are three members of the YHA, probably from Stoke-on-Trent Local Group, arriving for the night.

Right: The only known photograph of the hostel's traditional YHA sign, with Pauline James (née Habberley) enjoying the moment with Robert Hulme. The youth hostel had accommodation for 50 men and 50 women. The managers (or wardens) were Mr & Mrs Stanley.

Bygone Ipstones

These cottages (of which there were probably seven), were situated at Consall Forge approximately where the pub car park is situated. Note the tidy front garden to the surviving cottage above the canal. There was also a Methodist Chapel nearby.

Looking down Brookfields Road to the Sea Lion Inn in Edwardian times.

Village and other scenes

Hampton Villa on the corner of Belmont Road. The Froghall road has since been widened and a footpath added.

An Edwardian view of High Street with Beard's shop. It would be interesting to know the age of this building and why it is offset to the road.

Bygone Ipstones

Above: The village shop and below a procession outside the shop with the Marquis of Granby Inn in the background. Note the dogcart outside the pub. Virtually everyone wears a hat or cap.

Village and other scenes

John Redfern, trading as grocer and outfitter, the son of Ralph Redfern, also a tailor.
See also p.43 for one of John's invoices.

The shop is Abberleys on the left. This was also th Post Office. It is now dwellings and the roof has been altered.

Bygone Ipstones

The church from the lane to the common. Of interest is the building on the far right of the picture. It has now been demolished.

A view of the church taken from the cemetery, probably 100 years ago. There are no trees in the lane and possibly the cottage now 58 Church Lane may not have existed.

Social Events

The Devil's Staircase on the footpath from Belmont Road to Consall Forge. The steps have since been replaced.

2. SOCIAL EVENTS

Left: Mr & Mrs Greaves of Belmont Hall (seated) with Nurse Dulson of Foxt (also seated) on their left. The children are Elaine Hidderley and Colin Snow. The event was the Agricultural Show.

Below: William and Edna Podmore (far left) of Consall New Hall at the retirement of Mrs Stubbs, infant teacher, in c. mid-1960s. The lady with the white handbag (3rd from right) is Mrs Dorothy Wood, a fellow teacher with Headmaster Derrick Smith, 4th adult from the left.

Social Events

The Ladies' Section of the British Legion on an outing to Wedgwood's Pottery in 1965.

The Frothblowers have been raising funds for charitable purposes for c. 50 years. Here is their flower show in 1965.

Bygone Ipstones

Raising funds for the Frothblowers outside the old post office, again c. 1965.

The Ipstones OSC Girls PE Squad at the Memorial Hall c. 1956.

Social Events

The Ipstones OSC had a series of plays after the last war in the Memorial Hall.
This one was in 1949 (above) and in 1951 (below).

Bygone Ipstones

These are thought to be the Youth Club dinner (?Xmas dinner), again in the Memorial Hall.

Social Events

The W.I. in 1962.

The W.I. exhibition at the Ipstones Show in 1965.

Bygone Ipstones

A Group meeting of W.I.s in the district with a contingent of Ipstones ladies present.

This is thought to be similar to the above.

Social Events

Is this a W.I. annual dinner, c. early 1950s?

Mr Roland Goldstraw (3rd from right), the village butcher in 1965, at a barbecue. The policeman is Mr Parker.

Bygone Ipstones

The 'Sillybillies' with 'Maurice and his Music' in 1965.

The Youth Club with Mrs Lowndes and some of the girls engaged in sewing, embroidery etc, in the early 1950s.

Social Events

Ipstones Football Club in the 1921-22 season.

Ipstones Cricket Club, with Mr Lowndes on the left. The men are outside the former pavilion built for the Festival of Britain in 1951. The site is now occupied by the new playgroup building.

3. ALL IN A DAY'S WORK

Fred Cope with the night soil cart prior to the building of the Sewerage Works in 1959 (see also p.38 below).

All in a day's work

White Chimneys Farm, near Sharpcliffe on Ipstones Edge with (L-R) Herbert Habberley, Felicia Berrisford and Isaac Berrisford.

(L-R) Tom Burndred, Fred Burndred and Herbert Habberley with a Derbyshire Stone lorry and float at Ipstones Carnival c. 1950. Tom and Herbert drove for the quarry and at the Carnival.

Bygone Ipstones

The Ipstones Home Guard "on manoeuvres".

Dr. Evison; he was the local doctor in 1965.

Nurse Dulson of Foxt.

All in a day's work

The local Observer Corp used to meet at its observer post and at the school. Here are two views of some of the men going about their duties at both places. Below; Mr F Stubbs (Chief Observer) with Observer G. Ratcliffe.

– 33 –

Bygone Ipstones

The fire brigade practising for a 'quick assembly' competition in c. 1965.

Staff at the school canteen, with Mrs Cope on the left and Mrs Alexander on the right.

All in a day's work

The former Co-op in Church Lane. Prior to this it was situated at The Grove, off the picture to the left. In 1965 the manager was Mr K Brookes, assisted by Mrs Barnett.

The interior of Alexander's grocery shop with Mrs Doris Alexander.

Bygone Ipstones

The former High Street Post Office with Mr Poultney behind the counter and Mr Ted Bunce, the postman.

All in a day's work

Left: Far left is Keith Wainwright at the Marquis of Granby, the licensee's son-in-law and barman for the night, 1965.

Right: Clarice Bradbury, licensee at the Red Lion, Ipstones Edge,

Left: Neil and Sheila Clowes at the Golden Lion, 1965.

Bygone Ipstones

The opening of the new sewerage treatment works by local councillors in 1959, with Cllr. Beresford opening the tanks. Council representatives spend many hours discussing all manner of issues. Sometimes the work can be very rewarding and at others, just the opposite!

All in a day's work

A series of old bills and receipts has survived which record details of some of the local tradesmen of past years. A few are reproduced here as a reminder of their activities.

```
                    IPSTONES,                          190
  Mr I Berrisford
      BOUGHT OF
              John W. Haywood,
                    GROCER,
      IRONMONGER AND GENERAL DEALER.

      ½ Ld Rd Corn              7.3
      5 st Flour                6 8
      2 oc Ind Meal             2.6
         pd                    16.5

                    Dec 14th 1901
                      JWH
```

Ipstones grocer John Haywood, in 1901. In 1906 he had the Ipstones corn and oil stores and this may be the place Cardings had in 1908 (see below).

James Clowes & Sons were builders, wheelwrights and blacksmiths of Basford. This receipt is dated 24th September 1898.

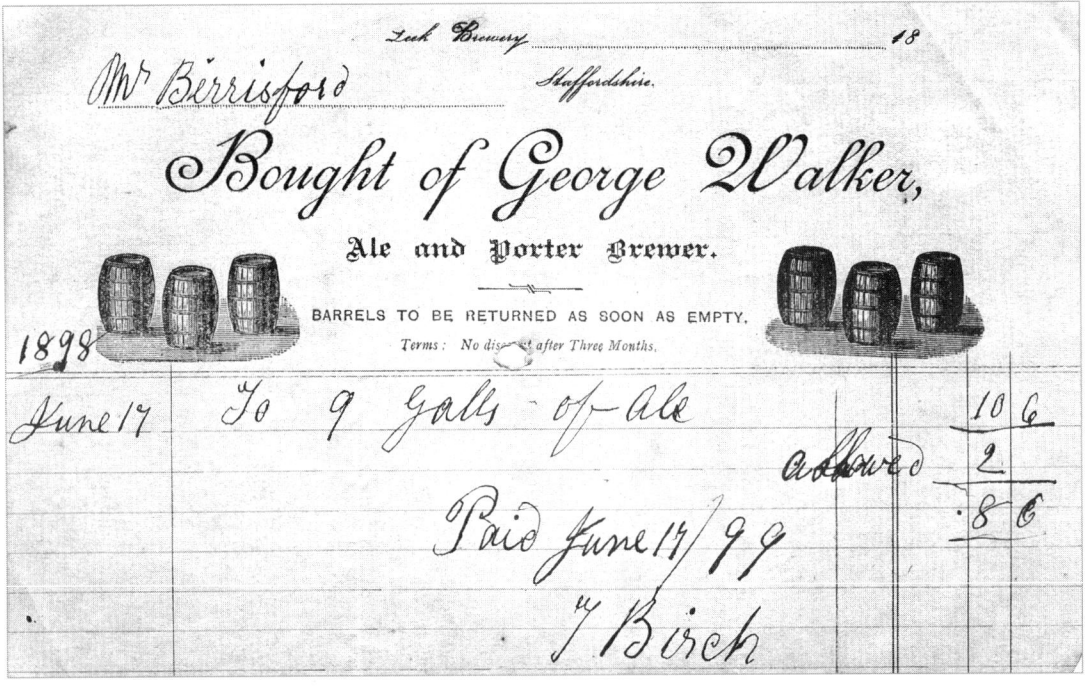

Nine gallons of ale bought by T. Birch and paid for on 17th June, 1899. They came from the Leek Brewery, run by George Walker. Note that the invoice is dated exactly one year earlier!

All in a day's work

This bill (above) is of Carding Bros., millers of Leek. However, it includes an illustration of their various mills. The top one is their Leek depot plus Ipstones Corn Stores, Winkhill Corn Mill and Waterhouses Corn Mill. The three stores are reproduced a little larger. The bill is dated 1908 and although the drawings are a little crude they are interesting, none-the-less.

Mosslee mill and house in 1927 when it was being sold as part of the Sharpcliffe Estate. The bill (below) shows that in 1896 the mill was occupied by John Bagnall.

All in a day's work

> Ipstones, Stoke-on-Trent,
> Ap 12-02 189
> Mr Isaace Beresford
> Bought of JOHN REDFERN,
> TAILOR AND CLOTHIER.
> CAPS, COLLARS AND TIES, ETC.
>
> 1902
> Jan Pr Cotton Cord Breeches & Legging   15 — 0
>
> Settled same time
> with thanks
> John Redfern

John Redfern, the village tailor supplied a pair of cotton cord breeches and leggings for 15s. 0d. (75p) in January 1902.

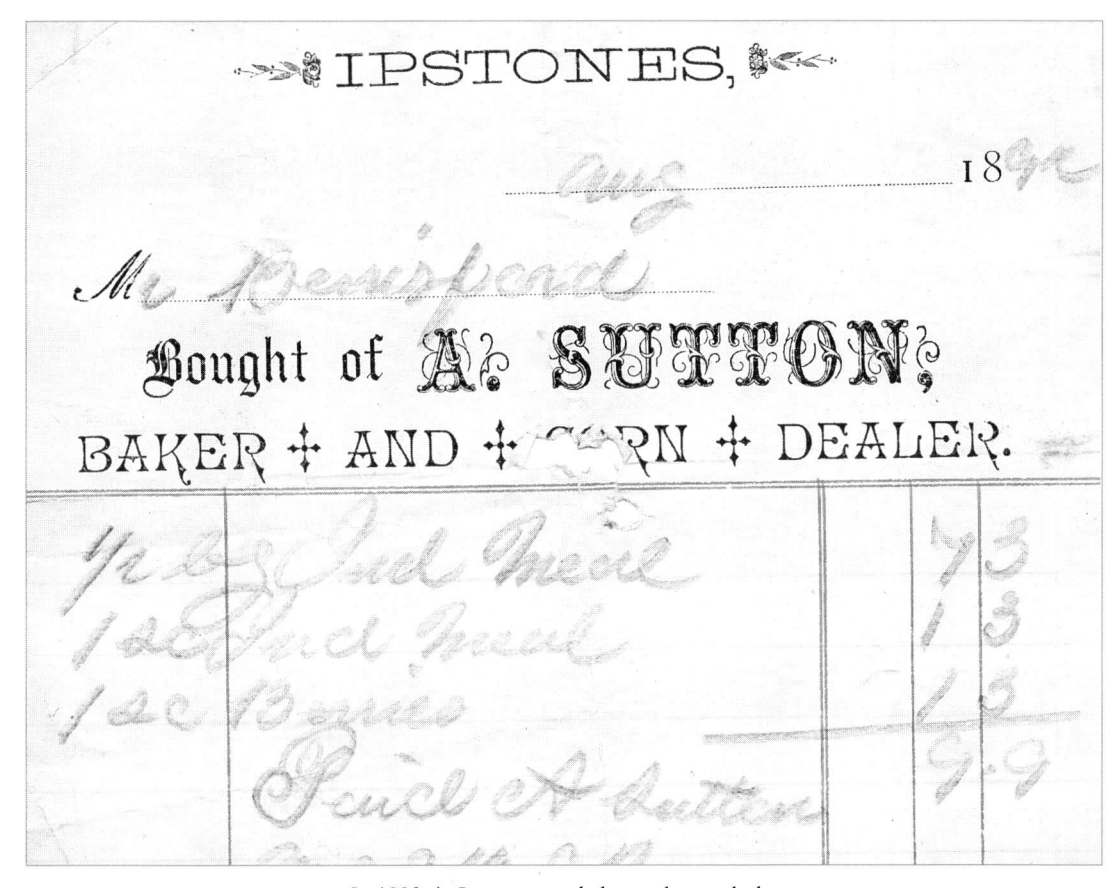

> IPSTONES,
> Aug 1892
> Mr Beresford
> Bought of A. SUTTON,
> BAKER AND CORN DEALER.
>
> ½ b Ind Meal   7 3
> 1 sc Ind Meal   1 3
> 1 sc Bran   1 2
>   9 9
> Paid A Sutton

In 1892, A. Sutton was a baker and corn dealer.

Mr Berrisford

Bought of:—

E. SCRAGG,
Grocer & Corn Dealer,
IPSTONES.

Always Drink BLUE CROSS TEA.
Fragrant & Delicious
Sold in Lead Packets & Decorated Tins

A LEADING LONDON TEA BROKER CERTIFIES:—
"I have again had samples of 'BLUE CROSS' TEAS submitted to me for critical examination. Having carefully tasted them, I confidently report that they are selected from the best gardens of Ceylon and India, are full and flavoury in the cup, and of high quality."

Date	Item	£	s	d
July 29th	½ bg Berries 6/6		6	6
	½ bg Indmeal 6/9		6	9
	1 bg Bran 10/9		10	9
		1	4	0
Aug 29th	Cash	1	0	0
			4	0
	Settled J. Sutton Sept 1st /01			

Dealing in corn was clearly a popular and apparently lucrative pursuit. E Scragg traded as a grocer and corn dealer in 1901.

All in a day's work

Various ladies with a common theme were photographed together at Above Church. The theme was that they were all in business on their own account. L-R: Helen Beaumont; June Brindley (post lady); Carol Goldstraw (mole catcher); Dorothy Gould (farmer's wife); Ruby Trafford (milk lady) and Dorothy Wood (school teacher). It was taken in 1965.

This image has caused your author some confusion in the past relating to its location. It is at Boltons at Froghall and the raised launder on the left carries canal water to a new brass works, when new foundations were needed for machinery. The floor was on made-up ground which caught fire. A photo in the *History of Thomas Bolton Ltd* shows the inner end of this launder, bringing the water to a large hole. At the rear (left) of the scene is a boiler and small chimney and a pipe leads away from it, presumably carrying hot water. In the centre, a vertical boiler powers the two rollers for crushing. Were Boltons making their own bricks? Possibly, for A S Bolton made his own bricks when he built his home at Moor Court, Oakamoor, in 1861. Alternatively it could be grinding ash/slag waste for the machine foundations. The date is c. 1910–12.

Bygone Ipstones

No. 43B—(Farmer).   DOGS.   No. 63/8

CERTIFICATE OF EXEMPTION FROM DUTY.
41 & 42 Vict., cap. 15.

I hereby certify that Mr. Isaac Berrisford, of Clough Meadows, in the Parish of IPSTONES, in the County of STAFFORD, has delivered a Declaration under the above-mentioned Act, stating that he is a **Farmer**, and that one Dog is kept by him solely for use in tending sheep or cattle on his farm, and I hereby further certify that he is exempt from Licence Duty in respect of such Dog while so kept and used until the 31st day of December next inclusive.

Dated this 12th day of JANUARY, 1897.

GEORGE RICHARDS, Supervisor of Inland Revenue.

NOTE.—This Certificate will become void and must be exchanged for a Licence if the dog ceases to be used for the purpose stated, or is used in taking rabbits or game, or, in the trade of a butcher or drover. A Declaration must be delivered and a fresh Certificate obtained in the month of January next, if required.

This Certificate must be produced, when required, to any Officer of Inland Revenue or Police, under a penalty of £5.

Many a farmer would no doubt feel lost without the assistance (and friendship) offered by his working dog. In the days of dog licences, working dogs were exempt. Here is a local dog licence exemption dating from 1897!

The Whiston Copper Smelter built by the Duke of Devonshire in 1770. It survived until c.1890 and it was demolished a few years later. The name Black Lane refers to the black copper slag used on the road in times gone by. The Duke sold the works in c. 1821 to John Sneyd & Sons, which would account for the Sneyds Arms name being in the plural.

— 46 —

4. VANISHED BUILDINGS AND WORKS

This pair of semi-detached houses existed by the canal at Froghall, opposite the portal to the tunnel.

Bygone Ipstones

Two more views of the same houses.

— 48 —

Vanished buildings and works

The Navigation Inn, which was at the roadside and opposite the houses above. Another building existed to the left of the inn and may be seen on p.61. This area of the canal was its terminus when it opened in 1777. The inn may well date from this time. When the canal was extended to beyond the Foxt road, no new inn was built at the new site. The scene with the dog shows the houses adjoining the inn. The dog used to sit on the wall waiting for a water-rat to swim by. It then launched itself down into the canal!

Bygone Ipstones

Froghall Mill, viewed from the River Churnet.

Vanished buildings and works

Froghall Mill in recent times.

Boltons taken from the Kingsley road, looking towards the Ipstones road that is just visible. This view would appear to show the mill and chimney on the left shortly after it was completed.

Bygone Ipstones

The works from nearer the road bridge over the railway and river.
The near buiding was the work's canteen and billiard hall.

Unfortunately, this image is out of focus, but is included because of some of the buildings which may be identified. To the right of the smoking chimney is the Navigation Inn and between the two are the two houses shown above (see pp 47–8). Below and facing the camera, to the right of the Inn is a house with two gables. Was this the manager's house, later demolished for factory extensions? It was known as The Coffee House and used as offices prior to demolition. Behind it is the Ipstones road dropping down to the Kingsley-Whiston road (far right). At this junction you can just make out the toll house. Note also the former kink in the A52 road at this point.

Vanished buildings and works

This interesting view of Boltons, taken from the Whiston Road shows a lot of properties now gone. Note the Navigation Inn on the far right. All the buildings in the middle of the scene have gone, some, but not all, finally being removed in 2008. In the foreground, the spur from the railway still leads up to the canal wharf. An interesting feature, also now removed, is the bridge over the Clough Brook near the bottom and left of centre. The house still survives in the foreground, but has been empty for a few years.

Finally, a close up view of some of the buildings near the far end of the site, these were demolished in 2008.

Bygone Ipstones

Podmore's flint mill, Consall Forge, in 1935. Most of these buildings survive, although the long shed has gone. There was another flint mill adjacent to this one, in the grassed area between these buildings and the iron cross-over canal bridge. A narrow boat is tied up by the mill and is probably Podmore's own boat *n.b. Perpetual*.

Note that the wood on the left now carries far more timber. About a third of the way up the wood is an old tramway which is just visible running above the river. Much of it has fallen away now and you'd have a job to see where it went. It is seen on p.70.

A view from 1935 towards Consall Forge showing Podmore's Mill. The cottages in the distance are probably the railway cottages near London Bridge.

Vanished buildings and works

London Bridge from Kingsley Far Banks. Much has changed on this scene. The canal and railway are now cloaked in trees. The house has been demolished and the circular road to the right of the house, turning towards London Bridge, has been replaced by a road bridge over the river, built by William Podmore. Above the house may be seen the former public road to Consall Forge. This was abandoned after a land slip in the wood caused part of it to fall away. A similar thing happened on the Ipstones-Foxt road near Clough Head Colliery.

The former blacksmith's forge, adjacent to the Sneyds Arms, at Whiston. Consall Forge was a different type of forge, used to produce iron bars for rolling into sheets at (the later) Podmore's mill site in the 16th century. The Sneyd family operated the Whiston copper smelter, buying it from the Duke of Devonshire in c. 1821. In 1846, they sold it to their manager, John Keys.

Bygone Ipstones

These final photographs show the former Cauldon Lowe Quarry which worked from the tramway from Froghall. This tunnel connected with another quarry.

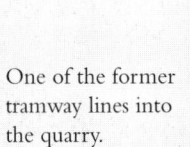

One of the former tramway lines into the quarry.

Stone was burnt to lime at Froghall in kilns and had been burnt at Cauldon Lowe by burning heaps of stone with wood. Here is one of the heaps. Regrettably all of these ancient remains of past industry have been swept away.

5. THE CANAL

This laden narrow boat (it is not a barge; although the owner was called a bargee) is full of limestone. The bargee will be by the horse, leaving his wife (under the bridge) and his daughter on the tiller. The boat, *n.b. Shannon,* is passing through floodgates which would be closed when the river beyond was in flood. The bridge is outside the Black Lion Inn, Consall Forge.

Bygone Ipstones

Another mother and daughter on a limestone boat, *n.b. Dora*. In both this and the previous scene, the daughters are wearing a shawl. The cottage on the left features also on p.55 for the boat is nearing London Bridge, Consall Forge.

Another view of the same boat in the last scene, this time near The Black Lion Inn, Consall Forge. She belonged to Price & Son of Brierley Hill.

The canal

Another scene of a loaded limestone boat, albeit of poor quality, with the horse ahead. In the 1850s 'four red boats and one white one' passed the Black Lion Inn 'every hour for ten hours a day'. The 'red boats' would be laden with Froghall ironstone, which was pillar box red (see also p.60). The white boats would be carrying limestone. If this oral tradition is correct, 50 boats a day would have been going up the canal and 50 laden boats returned, plus boats laden with coal leaving the area and other freight boats. The canal would clearly have been very busy.

This is *n.b. Edith* and unladen. She is heading for Froghall Wharf in all probability.

Bygone Ipstones

Mention above has been made about 'red boats', which carried Froghall ironstone. Here is what is believed to be one of these. It could have been coal, but much of the ironstone came from thin seams and many thin slabs can be seen in the boat, allowing the presumption of ironstone. The latter was valuable; ironstone needed calcium (eg limestone) in the smelting process, but Froghall ironstone's composition included calcium and the limestone was not needed. The boat is thought to be moored at Cherry Eye Mine's Wharf, which closed in 1923.

Opposite page: Hand pulling the maintenance boat from the tunnel entrance at Froghall. The building was just above the Navigation Inn.

The canal

Bygone Ipstones

Froghall tunnel framing a narrow boat just leaving.

The canal

These workers are looking down onto the canal at Foxt Road. Presumably they loaded stone onto the narrow boats.

A quiet day at Consall Forge.

Bygone Ipstones

Above: Consall Forge c. 1960. The footbridge no longer survives across the river.

Left: A sad scene c. 1960 of Froghall Wharf prior to restoration. Below: Nearby, a boat lies rotting in the canal.

The canal

These twin chimneys at Boltons were an impressive sight at Froghall.

A traction engine by the Consall Forge limekilns. The photograph was taken by William Podmore.

6. THE RAILWAY

In addition to the standard gauge railways (down the Churnet Valley and from Leekbrook to Waterhouses), there were several other railways and horse-drawn tramways. Here are a few scenes of one or two of them. They served quarries (the Cauldon Lowe Tramway, which confusingly became a cable drawn railway); coal and ironstone mines.

Above: The North Staffordshire Railway was unique in that it operated with three gauges of line: standard; 30inch (Manifold Valley Light Railway); and the Cauldon Lowe tramway's 3ft 6in gauge. Here is the latter worked with twin tracks but with a communal middle rail. Wagons descending drew up empty wagons as they were both on the same cable which ran from Froghall Wharf to Cauldon Lowe. This scene shows the line heading for Windy Harbour from Cauldon Lowe. The latter's spelling in this form goes back to at least 1785 in Chatsworth's Ecton Mine Accounts. See also pp. 71–2.

Right: Another view of a descending wagon with a man riding the wagon. This practice was illegal for safety reasons.

– 66 –

The Railways

One of the saddle tank locos that worked in the quarry. It was called 'Toad'.

Bradnop Station, c.1904, with a train to Waterhouses.

Bygone Ipstones

The valley side above Podmore's Mill below Consall Forge and its continuation north-west is known as Kingsley Far Banks. There were five levels working Froghall ironstone here, owned by W E Bowers. The wagons descended a cable-hauled tramway from 'Kingy's Drum' to the wharf by Podmore's Mill. It crossed the River Churnet and the Churnet Valley line on a spindly wooden-built bridge, shown here. It was 255ft long.

The Railways

The Manifold Valley Light Railway opened in 1904 but the connecting line to Leek was not finished. Construction work was carried on at both ends, using the narrow gauge locos at the eastern end. Here is perhaps the only photograph showing this. The loco is by the bridge over Earlsway Lane from Waterhouses to Cauldon Lowe.

Photographs of the mines at Ipstones and their tramways are not known, but perhaps some lie in an unknown prospectus or two. Here is a view of Cheadle Park Colliery, which opened in 1887. Three lengths of line can be seen and the tramways from other collieries in the area would have used similar rails and guage.

Bygone Ipstones

The tramline beneath Raven Rocks, opposite Podmore's Mill, Consall Forge, which went down the valley to Hazelwood Mine. A lot of this has fallen away in the last 50 years to the extent that it is difficult to follow its course.

A view of the former BICC (British Insulated Callanders Cables) sand quarry siding near Oakamoor in the early 1970s.

The Railways

Above: Across this field is a distinct area of grass on better drained land. It is the 1777 tramway at Windy Harbour (see below).

Right: The tramway to Cauldon Lowe from Froghall Wharf dates from 1777. It is the second oldest in the country and the oldest using iron rails to be created under a legislative enactment. Four different lines were used from 1777 to 1920, when it closed. A couple of features of the original line survive together with details of the rail itself.

At Froghall if you walk from the wharf along the footpath up the cutting of the railway you reach a path to the left which goes into the wood.

It is a nature reserve and the path (sometimes rather muddy) leads down to a little bridge over the brook. This bridge was built to carry the tramway. It is at Grid Ref: 032 480 The path then carries on up the valley-side to reach the road to Foxt.

At Windy Harbour, at the cross roads on the Froghall-Ashbourne road (A52) and the road from Leek to Ellastone, if you turn towards Ellastone and stop by the first gate on the left, you can see the 1777 tramway. The field is poorly drained, with an area of sedges and the tramway crosses the sedges.

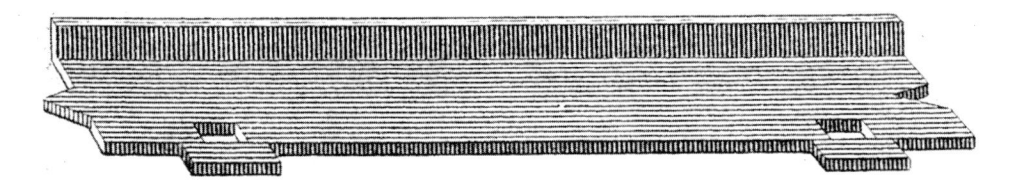

Above: The original tramway was made of wooden rails laid on wooden sleepers. On top of the wooden rails were attached 3ft lengths of cast iron rail, being 1¾in thick. A drawing of one of these survives in *Camden's Britannica* (under canals). The connecting nibs, the area of the hole (which took a wooden pin) and the flange which contained the wheels often snapped. Accidents were common as a result. The wagons at this time were horse-drawn.

A train accident at the Bolton Works, Froghall, c. late 1950s. Three wagons contained crates of whisky. Unexpectedly, most of it disappeared in the crash. The engine was seen to be glowing red hot and high speeds between Consall Forge and Oakamoor were common.

7. WINTERY REMINDERS

A few reminder of days gone by when the snow always seemed to lie deeper and for longer.

Church Lane in the 1960s, before the road was widened.

Brookfields Road.

Bygone Ipstones

Two more scenes in Brookfields Road in the early 1930s.

Wintery Reminders

The long and savage winter of 1947 brought havoc to the area and the aircrash in February on Grindon Moor of a mercy flight which claimed eight lives. Here is a scene in Leek Road near Bradnop a few days after the crash.

8. WHEN WE WERE YOUNG

An early photograph of Ipstones school, probably in Edwardian times

Opposite page: Ipstones school children in the 1934-35 year.

When we were young

Bygone Ipstones

Mrs Wood with one of the classes in the late 1940s.

Mrs Wood with the school's upper class in c.1949.

When we were young

Mrs Wood with the class of 1952.

Mr Butterworth with the school football team in the mid 1950s.

Bygone Ipstones

Mrs Wood with two sewing classes, c. 1968.

When we were young

The Mount Pleasant Methodist Church Christmas party, in 1965.

This is thought to be another Methodist Church party, probably at Christmas time.

Bygone Ipstones

The Methodist Chapel Youth Club, directed by Mr Hawkins, at their production of 'The Story of Christmas in Mime' in 1965.

The school dance team with tambourines on the recreation ground in 1950.

When we were young

1935 sports trophy winners. The trophies were presented by Sir Joseph Lamb.

A school nativity play at the village hall in the late 1950s–1960 period.

Bygone Ipstones

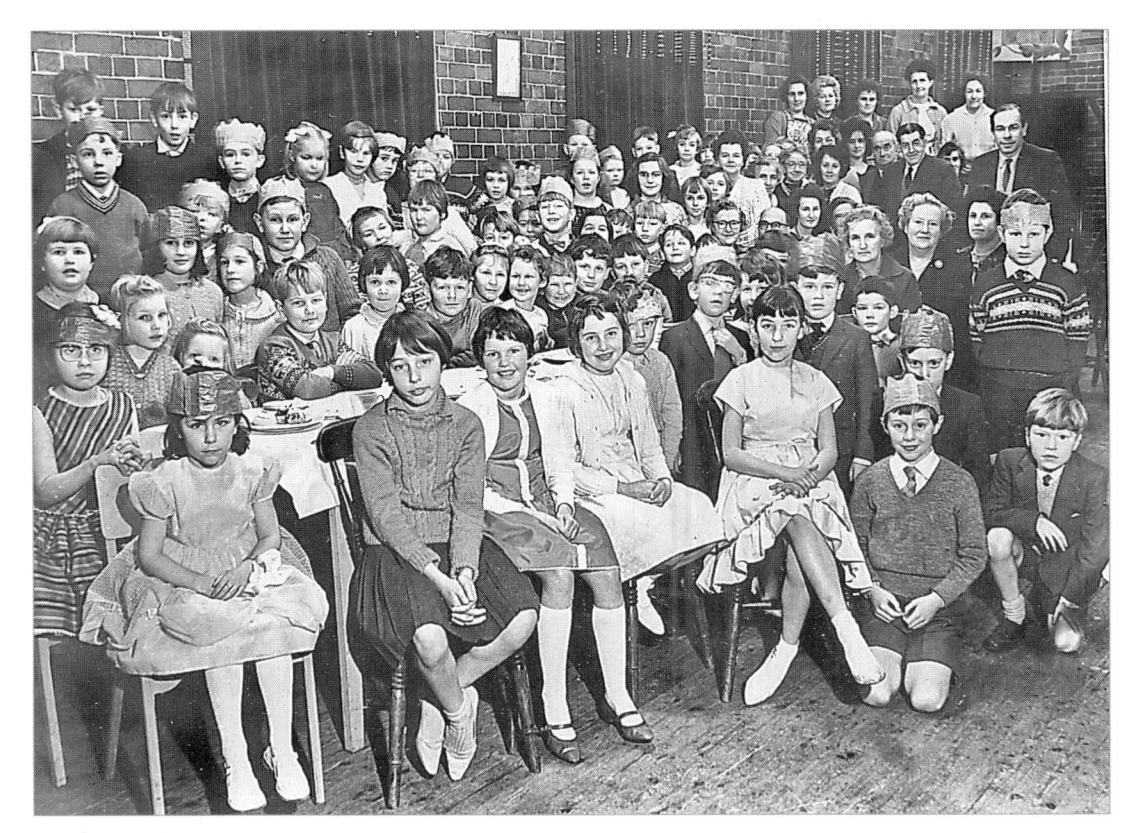

Possibly the school Christmas party, c. early 1960s.

The Nativity play, performed by school children at the church in the late 1960s-early 1970s.

When we were young

A school dance troupe of girls on the recreational ground. With parents watching, this could have been at the carnival.

Girls maypoling at the 1965 Ipstones Show.

Ida Barks c. 1933. The Queen the year before was Eileen Rudd, the year after Nina Jones.

When we were young

Lucy Goldstraw c. 1940. The carnival was cancelled due to the war!

Bygone Ipstones

School Carnival Queen Nellie Burndred pictured on the recreation ground in the 1940s.

When we were young

Pauline James (née Habberley) Show Queen in 1964. She is with her retinue and parents Becky and Herbert Habberley.

Margaret Burnett, (née Trafford) the Show Queen in 1970.

Bygone Ipstones

Gwen Richardson was the Show Queen in both 1960 and 1961. In 1960, she was presented with a cup by Harold Davies, M.P. when she was chosen as Queen of Queens at Churnet Hall, Cheddleton.

Above: Emma Hewson, Show Queen in 2005 with her retinue. Opposite page: Emma with her parents Sue and Paul.

When we were young

Jessica Bond, giving her retiring speech at the 2005 Show.

Jane Shemilt's wedding to Robert Grindey on 1st July 2000, the last parish wedding of the millenium.

When we were young

Susan Bennison's wedding to Jonathan Gould on 16th October 1999 is believed to be the penultimate wedding.

When your author was young, he had a desire to find Price's Cave near the Devil's Staircase, with its 200 steps to Consall Forge. He found it in June 2009! Traditionally a butler from Belmont Hall hid here from creditors. It is shown on the 1880 OS Map, but has an arched, cutstone roof. This would seem to indicate that it was built as a feature on the estate, perhaps by John Sneyd in the late 18th century. A walk for promenading from the hall existed above the cave and the wood and cliffs. It then returned to the hall above Crowgutter wood.

INDEX

A
Alexander's grocery shop 35

B
Beard's grocers shop 6
Belmont Hall 20
Belmont Road 15, 19
Black Lion Inn 57, 58, 59
blacksmith's forge 55
Boltons 45, 51, 53, 65
Bradnop Station 67
British Legion 21
Brookfield Road 8

C
Carding Bros 41
Carnival 31, 88
Cauldon Lowe Quarry 56
Cauldon Lowe Tramway 66
Cheadle Park Colliery 69
Cherry Eye Mine's Wharf 60
Church Lane 9, 10, 18, 35, 73
Clowes & Sons, James 40
Co-op 35
Consall Forge 14, 19, 54, 55, 57, 58, 63, 64, 65, 68, 96
Consall New Hall 20
corn dealer 43, 44
Country Store 7

D
doctor 32
dog licence 46

F
Foxt Road 63, 96
Froghall 7, 15, 45, 47, 50, 51, 56, 59, 60, 62, 64, 65, 66, 68, 71, 72
Froghall Mill 50, 51
Froghall tunnel 62
Frothblowers 21, 22

G
Golden Lion Inn 7

H
Haywood, John 39
Hazelwood Mine 70
High Street 11, 15, 36, 96
High Street Post Office 36

I
Ipstones Corn Stores 41
Ipstones Cricket Club 29
Ipstones Football Club 29
Ipstones Home Guard 32

K
Kingsley Far Banks 55, 68

L
Leek Brewery 40
London Bridge 54, 55, 58

M
Manifold Valley Light Railway 66, 69
Marquis of Granby 9, 16, 37
Memorial Hall 22, 23, 24
Methodist Church 81
Mosslee mill 42

N
Navigation Inn 49, 52, 53, 60
night soil cart 30
Nurse Dulson 20, 32

O
Observer Corp 33
OSC Girls PE Squad 22

P
Podmore's flint mill 54
Post Office 8, 17, 36

R
Raven Rocks 70
Redfern, John 17, 43
Red Lion 37

S
sand quarry siding 70
Scragg, E 44
Sea Lion Inn 14
sewerage treatment works 38
Sharpcliffe Hall 12
Show Queen 89, 90
Sillybillies 28
Sneyds Arms 46, 55
Sutton, A. 43

T
The Coffee House 52
The Linden Tree 7
tramway 54, 56, 66, 68, 71, 72

V
village tailor 43

W
W.I. exhibition 25
Waterhouses 41, 66, 67, 69
Waterhouses Corn Mill 41
Whiston 46, 52, 53, 55
White Chimneys Farm 31
Windy Harbour 66, 71
Winkhill Corn Mill 41

Y
Youth Club 24, 28, 82
Youth Hostel 13

Published by
Landmark Publishing Ltd,
Central Unit, The Oaks, Moor Farm Road West, Ashbourne, DE6 1HD
Tel: (01335) 347349   Fax: (01335) 347303   Email: landmark@clara.net
web site: www.landmarkpublishing.co.uk

1st Edition

ISBN: 978-1-84306-481-7

© **Lindsey Porter 2009**

The rights of Lindsey Porter as author of this work has been asserted by him in accordance with the Copyright, Design and Patents Act, 1993. All rights reserved. No part of this publication may be reproduced, stored in a retrieval system or transmitted in any form or by any means, electronic, mechanical, photocopying, recording or otherwise without the prior permission of Landmark Publishing Ltd. British Library Cataloguing in Publication Data: a catalogue record for this book is available from the British Library.

Print: Athenaeum Press, Gateshead
Design: Mark Titterton

Front cover: White Chimneys Farm, near Sharpcliffe on Ipstones Edge with (L-R) Herbert Habberley, Felcia Berisford, Isaak Berisford.
Back cover Top: A traction engine by the Consall Forge limekilns.
Back cover Bottom Left: An Edwardian view of High Street with Beard's grocers shop.
Back cover Bottom Right: These workers are looking down onto the canal at Foxt Road, Froghall.
Page 3: Heading for home.